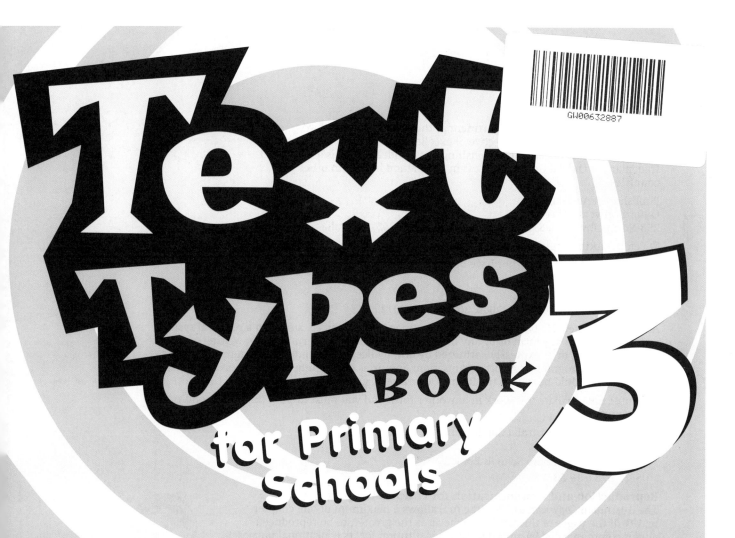

Text Types

Book 3

for Primary Schools

Second Edition

Peter Durkin • Virginia Ferguson • Geoff Sperring

OXFORD
UNIVERSITY PRESS
AUSTRALIA & NEW ZEALAND

OXFORD
UNIVERSITY PRESS

Oxford University Press is a department of the University of Oxford.
It furthers the University's objective of excellence in research,
scholarship, and education by publishing worldwide. Oxford is a registered
trademark of Oxford University Press in the UK and in certain other
countries.

Published in Australia by
Oxford University Press
253 Normanby Road, South Melbourne, Victoria 3205, Australia

© Peter Durkin, Virginia Ferguson and Geoff Sperring 2006

The moral rights of the author have been asserted

First published 2001
Second edition published 2006
Reprinted 2007 (twice), 2008, 2009, 2010, 2011, 2012

National Library of Australia Cataloguing-in-Publication data

Durkin, Peter
Text Types for Primary Schools Book 3
ISBN 978 0 19 555547 9

Second edition illustrated by Luke Jurevicius
Cover illustration by Nick Diggory
Typeset by watershed art and design
Printed in Hong Kong by Sheck Wah Tong Printing Press Ltd

Contents

Introduction

Text Types for Primary Schools, Second Edition, develops students' knowledge and understanding of texts and how they are structured. This knowledge will help students to create different spoken and written texts, as well as to interpret and respond more effectively to varied texts they will encounter throughout their lives. The text types highlighted in this series are stressed in all current state curriculum documents.

The series consists of seven consumable student workbooks, a *Starter Book* and Books 1–6, which each provide 26 units of work for use in teaching specific text types. Each unit consists of a double-page spread which includes text models and space for the student to practise writing in the text type.

All books in this series cover the following text types:

Factual texts	Literary texts
recount	narrative
transaction	information narrative
report	poetry
procedure	
persuasive	
explanation	
biography	

The books have been designed to give students the opportunity to practise writing over an extended period. Thus, three or more units are generally dedicated to each text type. These are presented in developmental order, from least challenging to most challenging.

How to use this book

Before beginning the activity, extensive discussion should take place.

The following teaching techniques should be incorporated into each unit's work, in order to maximise benefits from the modelled text types:

- **Model** the text type—by showing and sharing how writing is devised.
- **Discuss and display** what the students need to learn next; for example, how to gather and sort information.
- **Show** how text types can be linked and compared; for example, by recognising similarities and differences between text types. Once students understand the fundamental characteristics of a specific text type, they are better prepared to practise writing in the specific text type.

FT PAGE

odel page

monstrates
ecific text
e.

RIGHT PAGE

Activity page

Provides space
for students to
practise the
text type.

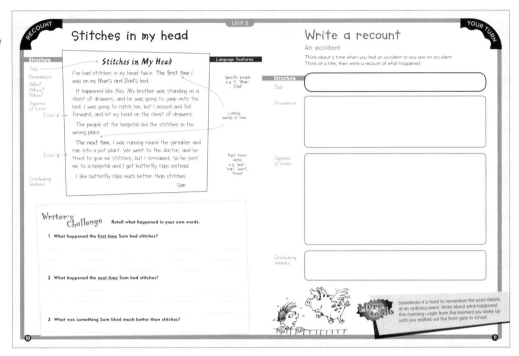

The activities throughout all books allow students to develop the following skills, which are critical in the writing of text types:

- observation—describing what one sees
- listening—to instructions and other students' opinions
- memory—recalling what one has learnt
- questioning—asking questions of oneself and others
- thinking—working out problems
- transference—transferring knowledge from one text type to another
- cooperative skills—working within a group.

Assessment

Each book incorporates a strong assessment component, in order to allow for self-assessment and teacher assessment of individual students:

- Student self-assessment page—allows students to assess their own understandings, knowledge and skills in writing specific text types.
- Student progress chart—helps the teacher keep track of the student's work, and is a valuable assessment tool.

Scope and sequence chart
BOOK

TEXT TYPE	UNITS

Recount

A recount records a series of events in the order in which they occurred. It tells how, what, where and when. Examples of recounts include:
▲ diaries
▲ letters/postcards
▲ journals
▲ autobiographies and biographies.

1   A visit to the zoo
2   Stitches in my head
3   A school excursion: the bird-walk
4   The day our duck egg hatched

Transaction

A transactional text is used to sustain relationships and involves simple interactions and negotiations, often in the form of letters, cards and invitations.

5   A letter to the Kids' Council

Report

A report classifies and describes general classes of phenomena.

A report is accurate and factual, and uses clear, straight-forward language.

6   Sharks
7   Dinosaurs
8   Polar bears
9   Bread
10 Our axolotl

Procedure

A procedure tells how to achieve a goal or an outcome through a sequence of steps. Examples of procedures include:
▲ instruction manuals
▲ recipe books
▲ safety manuals
▲ science books.

11 Making a pizza
12 How to make mud pies
13 How to make pepper jump

Persuasive text

A persuasive text persuades the reader to agree with a point of view.
Examples of persuasive texts include:
▲ advertisements
▲ pamphlets
▲ references
▲ posters
▲ book and film reviews.

14 Homework! Yes or no?
15 Cats make good pets
16 Poster: Cracklin' burgers

TEXT TYPE	UNITS
Explanation An explanation describes in scientific terms how natural and technological phenomena come into being. Explanations add to our store of knowledge.	**17** Why can you see your breath on a cold day? **18** Why do moths flutter around lamps? **19** What are fossils?
Biography A biography provides life details of a person, usually presented in chronological order. A biography includes precise details about birth place, and birth and death dates.	**20** Alice Grant: circus star
Narrative A narrative tells a realistic or imagined story. It is written to entertain, stimulate, motivate, guide and teach the reader. Examples of narratives include myths, legends, fables, fairy tales, short stories and picture books. Structure: ▲ Orientation (setting the scene) ▲ Complication (problems/conflict) ▲ Series of events ▲ Resolution (solution of problems) ▲ Re-orientation/coda (optional)	**21** The ants and the grasshopper **22** Princess and Oink **23** The magic cloak: a folk tale from Norway
Information narrative An information narrative is written to entertain, inform, describe or extend the reader's imagination. Factual information is often woven into the structure.	**24** Nan
Poetry Poetry helps us to think about familiar things in different ways. It uses language, rhythm, rhyme and structure to capture the essence of a feeling, thought, object or scene. Forms of poetry include cinquain, haiku, limericks, diamante, lyrics, ballads, humorous verse.	**25** A poem about the senses **26** Things

RECOUNT

A visit to the zoo

Title

Orientation
Who? When?
Where? Why?

Sequence of events
(in order)

1

2

3

Concluding sentence

Author

A visit to the zoo

On Wednesday our class went to the zoo by train. At Loch we stopped to pick up Patrick and Sharon.

When the train pulled in at Flinders Street station, we went straight to the Melbourne Zoo. As soon as we arrived we had lunch.

Then we went to see the lions, and they were all lying down having a rest.

After that we went down to the seals. They were all showing off.

Before we came home, Sister Eileen bought us all an icy pole.

David, Year 3

Time words
e.g. 'when', 'as ʃ
as', 'after' tell
happened ne:

Past tense
e.g. 'went', 'stopʃ
'arrived'

Writer's Challenge

Recounts tell about events in the order they happened. In the boxes below, draw pictures to match the labels.

1 We climbed on the train.

2 It stopped at the station.

3 Then we went to the zoo.

4 Next we saw the lions.

5 The seals were showing off.

6 Before we went home, we had icy poles.

Write a recount

An excursion

All recounts begin with an introduction (orientation) which tells who, what, where and when. Think of a time when you went on a visit or an excursion.

In the boxes below, write who, what, where and when about your excursion.

First, make notes about the excursion.

 Who?

 What?

 Where?

 When?

Write what happened next.

 Write a recount yourself. Write about a time when you went on a holiday with your family. Write an introduction (orientation) and then tell about all the events that happened. Draw some pictures as well.

RECOUNT

Stitches in my head

Structure

Title

Orientation

Who?
Where?
When?

*Sequence
of events*

Event 1

Event 2

*Concluding
sentence*

Language features

Stitches in My Head

I've had stitches in my head twice. The first time I was on my Mum's and Dad's bed.

It happened like this. My brother was standing on a chest of drawers, and he was going to jump onto the bed. I was going to catch him, but I missed and fell forward, and hit my head on the chest of drawers.

The people at the hospital did the stitches in the wrong place.

The next time, I was running round the sprinkler and ran into a pot plant. We went to the doctor, and he tried to give me stitches, but I screamed. So he sent me to a hospital and I got butterfly clips instead.

I like butterfly clips much better than stitches.

Sam

Specific people
e.g. 'I', 'Mum',
'Dad'

Linking
words of time

Past tense
verbs
e.g. 'was',
'ran', 'went',
'tried'

Writer's Challenge

Retell what happened in your own words.

1 What happened the <u>first time</u> Sam had stitches?

_____

_____

_____

2 What happened the <u>next time</u> Sam had stitches?

_____

_____

_____

3 What was something Sam liked much better than stitches?

_____

Write a recount

An accident

Think about a time when you had an accident or you saw an accident.
Think of a title, then write a recount of what happened.

Structure

Title

Orientation

Sequence of events

Concluding sentence

More to do

Sometimes it is hard to remember the exact details of an ordinary event. Write about what happened this morning—right from the moment you woke up until you walked out the front gate to school.

A school excursion: the bird-walk

Structure

Title

Orientation

Sequence of events

Concluding comment

Language feature

The bird-walk

When I was in Grade 3 at Everton Primary School, all the pupils had to go on a bird-walk.

The whole school had to trudge for miles up hills, across paddocks and along riverbanks, watching for birds.

Murray (my brother) and I hated bird-walks. Hated them! Every day we had to walk all the way to school and all the way home (about four miles). The thought of any more walking was terrible! So …

"There's a bird-walk at school tomorrow," we grizzled. "Can we stay home? Please!"

Mum agreed—it was a miracle!

We had a blissful "holiday", and just the thought of all the other kids walking and walking made us happier still!

Virginia Ferguson

Past tense word e.g. 'had'. 'hated 'thought', 'agree

Specific nouns 'Everton', 'pupi 'Murray', 'Virgir 'Mum'

Writer's Challenge

Recounts tell about events in the order they happened. In the spaces below, draw pictures with labels to show what happened.

Everton School bird-walk

Draw the children and teachers starting out, walking, searching, trudging, getting tired or going back.

Virginia and Murray's day

Draw them having fun, climbing trees, swinging, hiding or playing.

Write a recount

A special excursion

Write a recount about a special trip or excursion.

It could be:

- a visit to a special place
- your best holiday every
- the best party you ever had.

Structure

Title

Orientation

Sequence of events

Concluding comment

More to do

Have you ever been lost. Were you ever chased by a bull? Did you ever win a great prize? Were you a flowergirl or pageboy at a wedding? Choose something special that has happened to you and prepare a speech for your class.

RECOUNT

The day our duck egg hatched

Structure

Title

Summarises the text

Orientation

Tells who? where? what?

Sequence of events

Day 1

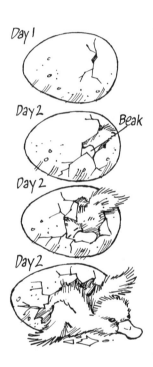

Day 2 — Beak

Day 2

Day 2

Conclusion

Language feature

The day our duck egg hatched

Our two duck eggs came from Susan's farm in Beechworth.

She brought them to our classroom, and we kept them in an incubator for 28 days.

Hatching Day 1. Monday 8.50 a.m.

One duckling was about to hatch out. There was a tiny crack in the shell.

Hatching Day 2. Tuesday 9.20 a.m.

The duckling made a hole in the shell with its beak.

Three and a half hours later (at 12.50 p.m.) the duckling's neck was tightly folded to fit inside the egg.

One minute later the duckling struggled out of the shell using big kicks. It was so wet and exhausted, we were amazed. Not one person spoke. We just stood and watched the poor little thing.

The duckling rested for a while, and soon its down (young feathers) started to dry out. It was cheeping softly.

We were quiet for the rest of the day. (We waited and waited but the other egg didn't hatch.)

Proper nouns (they begin with capital letters)

Time words Tell the exact order that things happened

Personal responses The writers say how they feel

Written in the past tens e.g. 'stood', 'spo 'watched'

Writer's Challenge

Look again at the 'Orientation' part of the recount to answer the questions below.

1 **Where did the duck eggs come from?** _____

2 **Who owned the farm?** _____

3 **How long were the eggs kept in the incubator?** _____

Write a recount

A special event

Write a recount about something special that you did or watched happening.
It could be:

- the day the chickens hatched
- taking the pet to the vet
- the day my baby brother or sister came home.

Structure

Title

Orientation

Who?
What?
When?
Where?

Sequence of events
Tell in the order they happened
Write about 3 or 4 events

Conclusion

Write a good ending sentence

More to do Write an eyewitness account. It could be something ordinary like a school sports event, or it could be something spectacular like a fire or an escaped animal.

A letter to the Kids' Council

Structure

Language feature

5 August

The President,
Kids' Council,
Everton Primary School

Dear President,
The girls in Grades 3 and 4 have formed a private club and we wish to ask permission to use a shelter-shed for our meetings.
We have tried other places, but the rain gets in and the boys wobble the walls.
The shelter-shed is sturdier.
Could you discuss this with the teachers and the Kids' Council and arrange to unlock the doors on our meeting days?
We promise to keep the place neat and tidy.
Thank you.

From The Girls of Years 3-4
Everton Primary School

Introduction
Tells the reader the topic

Argument
Stresses the writer's point of view

Concluding statement

Writer's details

Identifies parties involved

Sentence paragraph

Ends with a personal statement

Writer's Challenge

When you present a point of view in a letter, you need to set out clearly each argument. Think about the conditions at your school. Complete the sentences below:

Say what you need

At our school we need
_____
_____

Say why you need it

We need this because
_____
_____

Add another argument to support your point of view

As well as this
_____
_____

Write a letter

A letter to the Prime Minister

Write a letter to the Prime Minister about something you would like changed. Remember to include your point of view about what is wrong and why you want it changed.

Structure

Your address ⟶ _____
_____

Date ⟶ _____

Name of ⟶ _____
the P.M.

Prime Minister
Parliament House
Canberra ACT 2000

Name of ⟶ Dear _____
P.M.

I am writing to express my concerns about

Your point ⟶ _____
of view

(Say what _____
you think
should be _____
changed
and why) _____

_____

_____

_____

_____

Conclusion ⟶ _____

Good
finishing _____
sentence

Yours faithfully

Sign your ⟶ _____
name

If you are happy with the letter above, use it as a model to write a perfect copy to the Prime Minister. Post your letter and wait for the reply.

Sharks

A FACT CHART	**SHARKS**	

What kind of animal?
▲ sharks are fish
▲ they have large jaws and sharp teeth

• _____
• _____

What do sharks look like?
▲ they have smooth, tough skin
▲ they are grey-white or brown

• _____
• _____

Where do you find sharks?
▲ they live in oceans
▲ they sometimes swim in rivers

• _____
• _____

What do they eat?
▲ they are carnivores
▲ most eat live fish including other sharks

• _____
• _____

How does a shark move?
▲ sharks move very fast
▲ they use their fins and tails

• _____
• _____

How does a shark reproduce?
▲ in most sharks, the eggs hatch inside the females
▲ baby sharks are called pups
▲ the pups are born alive

• _____
• _____

A report

Sharks

Sharks are fish. They live in oceans all around the world. They have smooth, tough skin and are shaped like a torpedo. The streamlined shape helps them to swim swiftly.

All sharks are carnivores (meat-eaters). Their main prey is fish or other sharks.

Sharks differ greatly in size. Whale sharks—the largest fish of all—can grow up to 12 metres. The smallest sharks may measure 16 centimetres and weigh only 28 grams.

Many sharks are now protected because their numbers are falling rapidly.

Bundles of information

The first sentence descri[bes] what you are writing about

Concluding sentence

Writer's Challenge
After you have read more about sharks, add one or more facts to the boxes above.

Write a report

A FACT CHART   WHALES

What kind of animal?
▲ whales are mammals
▲ they live in water

- _____
- _____
- _____

What does it look like?
▲ they are very big
▲ they have a fish-like shape

- _____
- _____
- _____

How does it move?
▲ they use flippers
▲ they have a large tail which helps them move through the water

- _____
- _____
- _____

Where do you find whales?
▲ they live in oceans
▲ they can survive in both warm and very cold waters

- _____
- _____
- _____

Add more facts
Write your facts next to the dots

Now write a report. Use the information from the fact chart and facts from books and the Internet.

Structure

First sentence

Describe whales

Whales

_____

More to do

In your writing book, write a report on dolphins, or on a topic you are doing in class.

REPORT

Dinosaurs

Structure

Language feature

Title

General
statement

What kind
of animal

Description

Conclusion
Finishing
sentence

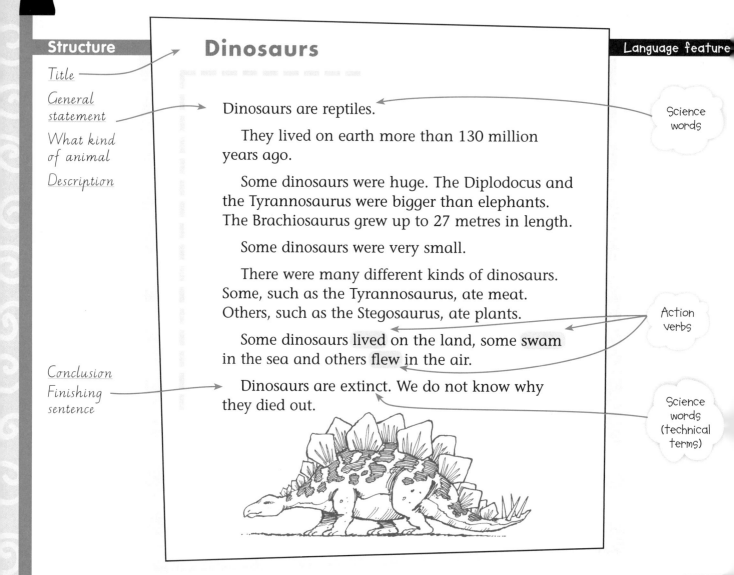

Dinosaurs

Dinosaurs are reptiles.

They lived on earth more than 130 million years ago.

Some dinosaurs were huge. The Diplodocus and the Tyrannosaurus were bigger than elephants. The Brachiosaurus grew up to 27 metres in length.

Some dinosaurs were very small.

There were many different kinds of dinosaurs. Some, such as the Tyrannosaurus, ate meat. Others, such as the Stegosaurus, ate plants.

Some dinosaurs lived on the land, some swam in the sea and others flew in the air.

Dinosaurs are extinct. We do not know why they died out.

Science words

Action verbs

Science words (technical terms)

Writer's Challenge

Reports contain science words. These are special words or terms used when writing a report. Use the dictionary to find the meanings of these science words.

1 extinct _____

_____

2 reptile _____

_____

3 dinosaur _____

_____

Write a report

Reptiles

Write your own report by filling in the gaps in the spaces below.

Title _____

General statement

Reptiles are scaly skinned animals. They are _____ blooded.

They need _____ sun to give them energy to _____.

Description

Types of reptiles

Write in different types

_____

_____

_____

Appearance

Reptiles are often covered in _____.

Fill in gaps

They shed their _____.

Tortoises and turtles are the only ones with _____.

shell

Sleeping habits

Some reptiles hibernate. (Look up dictionary to find meaning.)

That means _____

Eggs

Reptiles mostly lay _____ with a hard leathery shell. Some reptiles

hold their _____ in their bodies and give birth to live young.

Concluding sentence

Reptiles have been on _____

since the days of the _____.

Scales

More to do

Prepare a class report. Find out about one type of reptile—snake, crocodile, lizard or turtle. Make notes first, then present your report on a chart.

REPORT

Polar bears

Structure

Title

General statement

Description

1 Location

2 Appearance

3 Food

Conclusion

Language feature

Polar bears

Polar bears belong to the bear family.

They live in places like Alaska, Siberia, Norway, Sweden, Canada and other countries in the polar region.

The polar bear's coat is long and white. It has two layers. The fur underneath keeps the bear warm, and the outer coat helps it to shake off snow and water.

Adult polar bears weigh more than half a tonne. When they stand up they are nearly three metres tall.

Polar bears are carnivorous. Their main food is seals, which they catch through holes in the ice.

The polar bear is one of the biggest and most ferocious of all bears.

Action verbs e.g. 'live', 'shake' 'catch'

Diagrams

Science words

When they stand up polar bears are nearly 3 metres tall.

When they stand up polar bears are nearly 3 metres tall.

Writer's Challenge

Polar bears live in the polar regions. Use the report above and your atlas to complete the names of the countries below.

1 N___ ___ W___ ___
2 C___ ___ ___ D___
3 D___ ___ M ___ ___ K
4 R___ ___ ___ ___ A
5 G___ ___ ___ ___ L___ ___ D
6 A___ ___ ___ ___ A

Write a report

Bears

First decide which type of bear you are going to write about. It could be a grizzly bear, a brown bear, a panda bear or a teddy bear.

Find out all you can about the bear you have chosen. See if you can find a book about bears.

To write the report you can work with your teacher and other class members. Everyone can play a part in writing the report.

Structure

Title

The name of the bear

General statement

What type of animal is it?

Description

• *Describe its size, colour, appearance.*
• *Describe the food it eats.*
• *How does it catch its prey?*
• *When does it sleep?*
• *Does it hibernate in winter?*

Finishing sentence

Is it big, dangerous or frightening to people?

Diagram of the bear

More to do

With a friend, create a book list of bears. Read the books and find out all you can about bears. Make a class poster about bears, including illustrations.

REPORT

Bread

Structure

Title

General statement

Description

New paragraph for each new part of topic

Conclusion

Bread

Bread is our most important food. We eat it more often than any other food.

Bread gives us energy and helps us grow. It contains vitamins to keep us healthy, and minerals which are good for teeth and blood.

Bread is made from flour, water, salt, sugar and yeast. Most of the flour is made from wheat grain. (Grain is another word for seed.)

Here is a diagram of a grain of wheat. At the bottom is the germ, which is the part that grows into a new plant when it is planted.

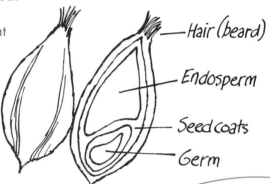

Grain of wheat

- Hair (beard)
- Endosperm
- Seed coats
- Germ

There are many types of bread available. These include white, rye, wholemeal and mixed grain breads.

Whether it's toast for breakfast or a sandwich or roll for lunch, most of us eat some type of bread every day of our lives.

Generic term e.g. 'bread', not type of bread

Technical language e.g. 'vitamins' 'minerals'

Use of timeless present tense

Topic Sentences tell wl the paragraph w be about

Writer's Challenge

Technical language

Most reports use technical language. Write at least 5 technical words from the report above.

E N ___ ___ ___ ___ ___ ___   M   G ___ ___ ___

M ___ ___ ___ ___   R ___ ___ S   Y ___ ___ ___ T

V ___ ___ ___ ___ ___ ___   N ___

Write a report

Food and drink

Choose a type of healthy food or drink, such as juice, milk, apples or butter, to write a report.

Use the books and computers in your school to help you locate the information you need.

YOUR TURN

For the teacher
The search for information could be done as a group or whole class exercise. Use wall charts.

Structure

Title

General statement (what kind of food)

Description
New paragraphs for each new part of the topic

Diagram

Write a concluding sentence or paragraph

More to do

Use what you have learnt about reports to prepare a report on a topic of your choice. Present it as a two-minute talk to the grade.

Our axolotl

Structure

Purpose
(to describe a
living thing)

Classification

Description
*What it looks
like*

What it eats

What it does

Conclusion

Language features

Our axolotl

Our class has an axolotl.
We have named her Alexia.

This is our report about our axolotl.

Axolotls are a type of salamander with red, feathery gills. The dictionary says, 'A newt-like amphibian'.

Appearance

Her head is flat with a black spot under her chin. Her tail is thin. She looks like this:

Size

She is 20 cm long, 2.5 cm wide (in the back) and 4 cm wide (in the head).
   She eats meal-worms and sometimes parts of other fish or axolotls. Sometimes she eats all of them! She can be a cannibal.

She shows three kinds of activity:
i   lying very still on the bottom of her tank
ii after being fed she becomes lively and turns somersaults
iii sometimes she swims round violently, thrashing the water with her tail, her head out of the water.

'Axolotl' is a Mexican word for 'play in the water'. It is a name that suits Alexia perfectly.

Describing words (adjectiv... e.g. 'feathery', 'r... 'newt-like', 'fla... 'thin'

Action words (verbs e.g. 'eats', 'sho... 'swims', 'play...

Writer's Challenge

Look back over the description to answer these questions:

1 How long is she? _____ cm

2 What does she eat? _____

3 Axolotls are a type of S_____

4 'Axolotl' is a Mexican word meaning _____

26

Write a report

Pets

Do you have mice, lizards, guinea pigs, tortoises, terrapins or chickens?
Tell us some facts about your pet or a friend's pet.

Structure

Classification

Description

1

2

3

4

5

*Interesting
fact*

Conclusion

Name of pet (kind of animal)

Your animal's first name

Colour

Size

Appearance (what it looks like)

Food

Behaviour (what he/she does. Playful? Quick moving? Slow moving? Habits)

One good thing you remember about this pet

More to do

In your writing book, draw a portrait of your pet. Draw a frame, print the name of your pet at the top and sign your name at the bottom. Display your picture in the classroom. Does your picture match the report of your pet?

PROCEDURE

Making a pizza

Structure

Title

Materials

List all of the ingredients for making the pizza.

Sequence of steps

Include picture or labelled diagram

Evaluation

Was your pizza cooked properly? Did you enjoy it? If so, your procedure was successful. Bon appetit!

Making a Pizza

You will need

▲ prepared pizza base   ▲ tomato paste

▲ shredded ham   ▲ grated cheese

▲ pineapple pieces

What to do

1 Spread tomato paste on the pizza base.

2 Sprinkle shredded ham over the entire surface.

3 Add pineapple pieces.

4 Cover with grated cheese.

5 Place in pre-heated oven (300°C) and cook for 20 minutes.

6 Cut into slices and serve with salad.

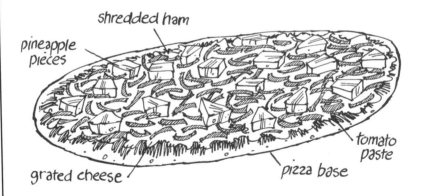

shredded ham

pineapple pieces

grated cheese

tomato paste

pizza base

Language features

Outline and number all the steps for making the recipe.

Recipes leave out all unnecessar words such as 'th 'and', 'them'

Writer's Challenge

Each of the 6 steps above begins with a verb (doing word). Several other verbs are also used. Write down eight verbs which appear in the sequence of steps. The exact space is given (one space for each letter). No word is repeated twice in this exercise.

S___ ___ ___ ___   S___ ___ ___ ___k___ ___

A___ ___   C___ ___ ___ ___

C___ ___   P___ ___ ___ ___ ___

Write a procedure

Making a salad sandwich

Write out all the steps for making and serving your favourite sandwich. You may like to use the pictures and words in the border to help.

YOUR TURN

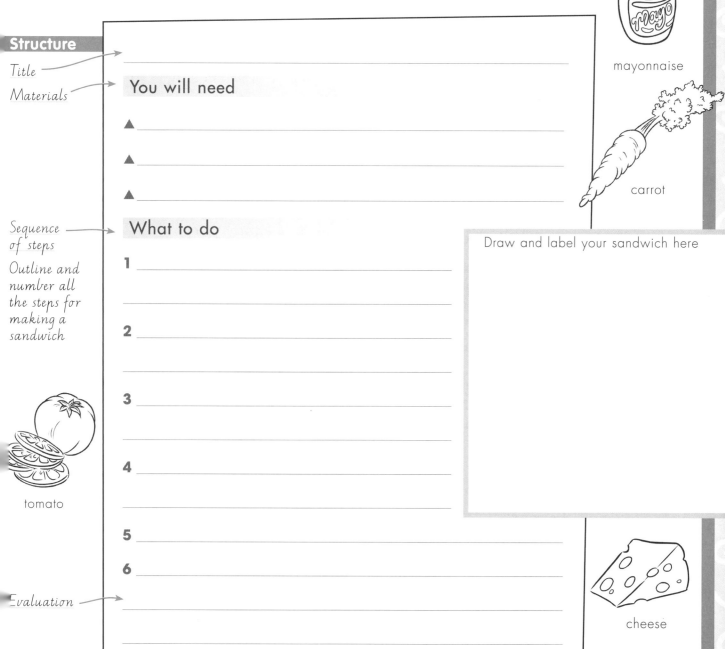

Structure

Title

Materials

You will need

▲ _____

▲ _____

▲ _____

Sequence of steps

Outline and number all the steps for making a sandwich

What to do

1 _____

2 _____

3 _____

4 _____

5 _____

6 _____

Evaluation

Draw and label your sandwich here

mayonnaise

carrot

tomato

cheese

lettuce   cucumber

More to do

Organise a healthy snacks day. Write out your favourite recipe, make it at home and bring it to school to share. Compile a recipe book of all the healthy snacks.

PROCEDURE

How to make mud pies

Structure

Title

The aim

Materials

Steps

Evaluation
If the mud pies set well and look delicious, then the recipe has worked!

How to Make Mud Pies

You will need

✓ an old plastic container
✓ an empty egg container
✓ water
✓ plenty of warm sun

What to do

1 Find an old plastic container.

2 Fill it $\frac{3}{4}$ full with rich dirt.

3 Add water and stir.

4 Pack this mud into the bottom part of an egg container.

5 Dry slightly in the sun.

6 Turn the carton over and leave the mud pie in a sunny place, without the mould.

7 When the pies are hard they are done.

If the pies are hard and they last for more than an hour or two, then the recipe has worked.

Action words at the start of each instruction

Numbers show order of steps
1 ....
2..............
3..............

Writer's Challenge

An important part of any procedure is evaluation. Evaluation is deciding whether the procedure worked or not. This evaluation gave reasons for why the procedure was successful.

In the spaces below, give four reasons why you should keep some mud pies in your cupboard.

1 _____

2 _____

3 _____

4 _____

Write a procedure

A bushland meal

For your recipe you could choose:

- a bark sandwich
- iced rainwater tea
- gumnut cider
- a work omelette
- roast rocks
- a recipe of your own.
- grilled mud sandwich
- moss custard

Structure

Title

You will need

Materials

What to do

>

>

>

>

Steps

Evaluation
Did it work?
How good was your recipe?

Work with your friends to plan a menu for a bushland feast. You will need to plan for breakfast, morning tea, lunch, dinner and supper. Copy the menu into your writing book.

PROCEDURE

How to make pepper jump

Structure

Title

Aim

Materials needed

What to do

Sequence of steps

Evaluation
Was the goal achieved?

A science trick

To take the pepper away from a pile of salt

> A dry winter's day
> a small pile of dry table salt
> some pepper
> a small comb

Wait for a winter's day

1 Make a small flat pile of dry table salt.

2 Shake some pepper on top.

3 Run a comb through your hair or rub it hard against your jumper.

4 Place the comb above the salt (without touching it).

5 The pepper grains will jump onto the comb.

> Facts
> Say exactly what is needed

> Action verbs
> 'make', 'shake', 'run', 'place'

If the pepper jumped onto the comb, your goal was achieved.

> Diagrams

PEPPER SALT

Writer's Challenge

Try this science trick for yourself, and then write exactly what happened. Did the pepper jump onto the comb?

Write a procedure

You can make balloons stick to things just by rubbing them. The pictures show you how. You write in the words for the procedure.

Balloon magic or Tricky balloons or Sticky balloons

Structure

Title .... **Balloon** ....

Materials needed

1 ....

2 ....

Sequence of steps

What to do

3 ....

First *Blow*

....

....

Second *Rub*

....

....

Next, take the b ___ ___ l ___ o ___ which has been

rubbed against material or your hair and given a charge of

st ___ ___ ___ c   el___ ___ ___ ___ ___ c ___ ___ y.

Put it on _____ and you will notice _____.

Evaluation   Was the goal achieved? _____

More to do   Tear up some paper into small pieces. Rub a plastic comb hard in your hair. Put it near the pieces of paper. The paper will jump onto the comb.

Homework! Yes or no?

Structure

Language feature

Homework! Yes or no?

NO

Introduction

I am in Grade 3 and I don't think children should get homework because they work all day at school and come home and have to do more work!

Arguments against homework

Also it creates homework for teachers because they have to go home and correct it.

Another thing is that mothers, fathers, brothers, sisters and friends have to help with homework, so **they** have extra homework as well.

Conclusion

As you can see, homework is unfair to many people. Children are too young to have such trouble. They should be able to play without worrying about homework!

– Alicia, Grade 3

YES

Introduction

I disagree with Alicia's opinion.

I know that it can be annoying to have to do homework when you feel like relaxing, but what about the future? Do you want a good job or will you turn into a lazy layabout?

Homework does three good things:

Arguments for homework

1 It gets you into the study habit so that it becomes a normal way of life—the more you do, the easier it becomes.

2 It revises the work you've done in school so you will remember it better.

3 There are so many things happening in schools that some basic subjects miss out. Homework gives us time to catch up.

Conclusion/ recommendation

I think Alicia should be more positive. Do your homework because you **want** to do it, not because you are made to. Remember, it will help you later on in life.

– Dimitri, Grade 3

Writer's Challenge

Should homework be set for children in Grade 3?

Give your opinions for and against.

YES	NO
I think homework **should** be given because:	I think homework **should NOT** be given because:
1 _____	1 _____
2 _____	2 _____
3 _____	3 _____

Write a persuasive text

Detention

Should children be kept in at recess?

Structure

Introduction

Arguments for

Arguments against

Summing up

Recommendation

More to do

Detention is banished. Think up four or five fair and effective punishments. Write them in your writing book.

1 If children are sloppy and messy.
2 If children are wild and noisy.
3 If children are teasing younger children.
4 If children are fighting in the yard.
5 If children are rude to adults on the way home from school.

PERSUASIVE

Cats make good pets

Structure

Language feature

Title

Your opinion

Arguments for

Arguments against

Conclusion

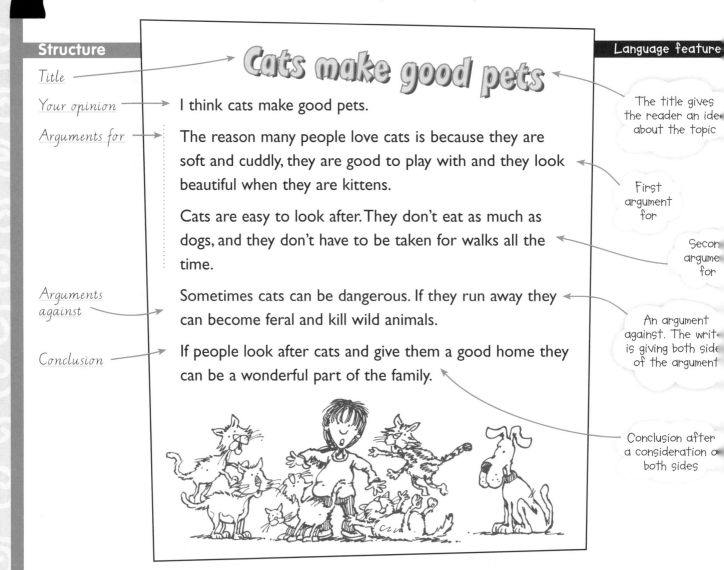

Cats make good pets

I think cats make good pets.

The reason many people love cats is because they are soft and cuddly, they are good to play with and they look beautiful when they are kittens.

Cats are easy to look after. They don't eat as much as dogs, and they don't have to be taken for walks all the time.

Sometimes cats can be dangerous. If they run away they can become feral and kill wild animals.

If people look after cats and give them a good home they can be a wonderful part of the family.

The title gives the reader an idea about the topic

First argument for

Second argument for

An argument against. The writer is giving both sides of the argument

Conclusion after a consideration of both sides

Writer's Challenge

Are you in favour of having cats as pets?
Write your arguments for or against cats in the space below.

_____

_____

_____

_____

_____

_____

Write a discussion

Structure

Title
Your opinion

Arguments for

Argument against

Conclusion

Dogs make good pets

I think

1 The reasons dogs can be good pets are because

2 Another reason dogs make good pets is because

A reason dogs might not be good pets is because

More to do In your writing book, write why a tiger or an elephant would not make a good pet, or why a rat might or might not make a good pet.

Poster: Cracklin' burgers

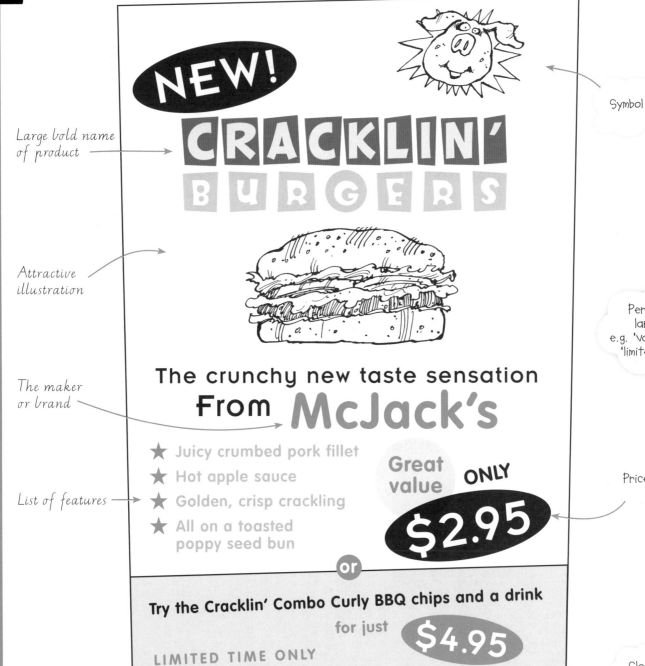

Large bold name of product

Attractive illustration

The maker or brand

List of features

Symbol

Persuasive language e.g. 'value', 'new' 'limited offer'

Price

Slogan

Writer's Challenge — Persuasive language

Advertising posters contain words that aim to 'sell' the product, or to persuade people to buy the product. Collect examples of persuasive language in magazines and newspapers. Select the best and make a huge wall poster for the classroom.

Design an advertising poster

Design an advertising poster for a new ice cream that you have created. Make it really different and original. Think about flavour, shape, size, packaging etc.

Write the name of your ice cream in large letters. Draw a bright, attractive picture of your product. Show the price clearly.

 **More to do**

Work with a partner to write a radio advertisement to sell your new ice cream. Rehearse it and record it on a tape recorder to play back to the grade. Really 'sell' the product.

EXPLANATION

Why can you see your breath on a cold day?

Structure

Language feature

Question in heading

> ## Why can you see your breath on a cold day?

Introduction tells about topic

If you go outside on a cold day and blow out your breath, you can see a small, steamy cloud in the air.

Words showing how and why e.g. 'if', 'when'

Explanation sequence

a series of points telling how and why

Your breath has moisture in it. Your breath is warm because the inside of your body is warm.

When you blow that moist, warm air into the cold, out-of-doors air, your breath suddenly cools.

Some of the moisture you have breathed out turns to water droplets. They form a small steamy cloud. This is called condensation.

Technical terms

Conclusion

A rounding-off sentence

If you breathe into your hands on a cold day, you can see and feel the moisture that forms on your hands.

Action verbs e.g. 'blow', 'breathe', 'see', 'feel'

Diagram

Explanations often have a picture or diagram

moist, steamy cloud

Writer's Challenge

In your own words

Explanations are written to help you understand how and why something happens. Show your understanding of this topic by writing a short explanation in your own words.

Write an explanation

Why is the ocean salty?

Use the fact file to write an explanation for why the ocean is salty.

Do not forget to do a labelled diagram.

Structure

Write a question in the heading

Introduction

Sentence that tells about topic

Explanation sequence

Write the facts in order so they tell how and why

Write a good conclusion

Fact file

- There is a lot of salt in the ocean.
- Salt is a mineral found in rocks and soil.

  When it rains, water picks up salt from rocks and soil and carries it to rivers.

  Rivers flow into the oceans and with them goes a little salt.

  This has happened for millions of years, and the ocean is now very salty.

More to do

Research funny and interesting aspects of the body, such as sneezing, hiccups, blinking, scratching, crying, smiling and burping. Choose people to write a short explanation for each topic, and make a Body Book for the grade to read and share.

Why do moths flutter around lamps?

Structure

Language feature

Question in heading

Introduction tells about topic

Explanation sequence

A series of points telling how and why

Conclusion

Diagram

Explanations often have a picture or diagram

Why do moths flutter around lamps?

We have all seen moths fluttering around globes and candles at night.

They do this because when they fly at night they use the light of the moon and the stars for navigation.

Bright lights such as globes and candles confuse them, and they lose their way. They circle and crash into the lamps, and may even burn themselves on the hot bulb or flame.

When the light is turned off or the candle blown out, the moths continue on their way.

Technical terms
Words showing how and why

Action verbs e.g. 'circle', 'crash'

Writer's Challenge — Finding the main points

There are two main points in the explanation above.
Find them and write them in your own words.

1 _____

_____

2 _____

_____

Write an explanation

How do spiders catch their prey?

Explanations tell you 'how' and 'why' about the topic.
Use the fact file to complete the boxes below.

Spiders

1 Write two facts about how a spider traps its prey.

_____

_____

_____

_____

2 Draw a diagram showing how a spider traps its prey.

Use labels

Fact file

The support lines are built first.

Radiating threads are laid next.

The spiral thread is laid last.

The spider detects the vibrations of trapped prey via a 'signal thread'.

Spiders

- Spider silk is as strong as steel thread of the same thickness, but is lighter and more elastic.
- Spiders mostly catch live insects.
- For many spiders, the web is both home and a food trap.
- In our climate (temperate) spiders usually live from one to three years.
- Web-spinning spiders pick up vibrations through the silk threads of the web. This makes it easier to catch insects because their eyesight is poor.
- Some web-spinners store insects to be eaten later. They cover their victims, dead or alive, in bands of silk.
- Spider silk is sticky. When an insect lands on the threads it is stuck!

More to do

Whole class activity. Use the facts you have written above to make a class wall chart on spider webs. Model the chart on the explanation about moths.

What are fossils?

EXPLANATION

Structure

Question in the heading

Introduction tells about topic

Explanation sequence

Facts in order— tell how and why

Conclusion

To sum up

Diagram

Labelled diagrams or pictures to explain topic

 What are fossils?

Fossils are the prints or parts of animals and plants that lived on Earth long ago.

Fossils help us to know what the plants and animals were like thousands of years ago. A fossil can be an animal that died and became trapped in sand, mud or rock. The soft part of the body rots, but the bones or skeleton becomes harder and turns to stone.

Some fossils are prints of a plant, or an animal or a shell. Sometimes living things fell into mud or tar and became buried. When the body rotted away a mould was left.

Scientists can fill the mould with plaster or plastic and make a cast of the animal.

Scientists who look for and study fossils are called palaeontologists.

Use of timeless present tense e.g. 'rots', 'becomes', 'turns'

Words showi how and wh e.g 'but', 'wh

Use of technical ter e.g. 'palaeontologi

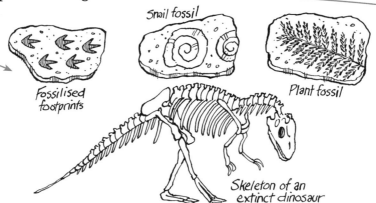

Snail fossil

Plant fossil

Fossilised footprints

Skeleton of an extinct dinosaur

Writer's Challenge — Technical terms

Explanations often use technical terms. Circle these technical terms in the explanation and find and write their meanings.

1 mould _____

_____

2 skeleton _____

_____

Write an explanation

Your own topic

Write an explanation about a topic that interests you.
It could be television, trucks, computers, rain.

Write your heading as a question

Introduction

Explanation sequence

Diagram

For the teacher

Students will need help before they begin this activity. An explanation could be modelled on a wall chart for the whole class. For example, 'rain', 'light bulbs'. Students might then work in groups to do research on their topic of interest before writing the explanation.

Conclusion

BIOGRAPHY

Alice Grant: circus star

Structure

Brief introduction

Date of birth

Early life

The times in which she lived

Career

Career highlight

Date of death

Tribute

Alice Grant: Circus Star

Some children dream of running away to join a circus, but for Alice Grant that was never a problem. She was born into one of the oldest and biggest circus families on 12 July 1910.

Alice's first school room was a circus tent. She had normal lessons but her real education was observing circus folk, animals and audience behaviour.

Throughout her life, she and her family moved from town to town, bringing the circus to people all over Australia.

The circus never stopped. It kept on playing right through two world wars and other troubled times.

Alice practised constantly and by the time she had grown up, she could do all the circus skills. She was an expert in acrobatics, juggling, riding and tightrope walking.

Old-timers still recall her most daring feat: a tightwire was strung between two huge buildings in Martin Place, Sydney. It was 40 feet above the ground! Alice calmly walked across.

She died on 4 April 2005, but her spirit will never die. It will live on in the lives of all circus lovers, and in the lives of her children, grandchildren and great-grandchildren, many of whom continue to follow in her footsteps.

> Past tense e.g. 'moved', 'stoppe 'walked', 'died'

> 'ING' words are used to give feeling c movement e.g 'observing', 'bringing', 'play 'juggling', 'ridi

> Exact dates must be used.

Writer's Challenge — About Alice

On another page:

Write a newspaper report of Alice's daring feat. Draw a sketch and write labels.

1 How old was Alice when she died? _____

2 What circus skills did Alice have? _____

_____

3 One of Alice's grandchildren wrote, "Alice was 39 going on 38." What does this mean?

_____

_____

Write a biography

Choose an older person whom you know well, such as a grandparent or neighbour. Interview them about their life. Make notes, check dates (birth, wedding etc.) and use photos if you can.

Begin simply, e.g.: <u>May Wood</u> was born in <u>Beechworth</u> on <u>1 January 1930</u>.

who?   where?   when?

Structure

Title

Person's name

When and where born

School

Early life

Early work

Wedding

Children names and dates

Later life

Make a class book called 'Grandparents'. Choose one of your grandparents. Do a short biography. Just facts (follow the simple structure above). Add a photo or sketch.

Collect the pages together and make into a class book.

The ants and the grasshopper

Structure

Language feature

A fable

Orientation

Telling when and why

It was a sunny spring day and the grasshopper sang with joy.

He looked down at some ants. They were working hard, looking for grain to take to the store.

"Poor things," he thought.

"Don't work so hard," he called. "Come and dance with me."

The ants kept on working.

Sequence of events

The plot in a fable is usually simple, and is based on the main event.

"If we don't work now, we'll have no food in the winter," they said.

"That's silly! Winter is months away. Surely you could dance for two minutes."

But the ants kept on working.

Months passed. It was a fearful winter and the grasshopper was so cold and hungry he could hardly move.

He trudged past the warm, cosy ants who were enjoying a feast. "Please give me some food!" he cried.

Resolution

The tale is written to teach a lesson or to make a point.

The ants kept on eating. "No," they said. "You sang and danced in the sunlight when you could have been working, so now you can shiver and starve in the snow!"

Happy words e.g. 'sun', 'spring' 'dance'

Repetition 'the ants kept on ...'

Very short sentences followed by a long one

Alliteration sounds pleasant and is easy to remember.

Writer's Challenge

Draw a before and after picture. One of spring, with the grasshopper dancing in the sun while the ants work busily, the other a winter picture with the ants warm and cosy and the grasshopper hungry and cold.

Before

After

Write a fable

An animal fable

Choose your animals and moral. Now write a story which shows that your moral is right.

Structure

Title

Orientation

Why? What? When?

Sequence of events

Don't forget a new paragraph for a new event

Resolution (concluding sentence)

Does your fable teach a lesson?

More to do

In your writing book, retell a well-known fable. It could be … slow and steady wins the race or 'Too many cooks spoil the broth'. Or choose one of these proverbs: 'Look before you leap', 'Don't be greedy', 'Don't show off', 'You can have too much of a good thing'.

NARRATIVE

Princess and Oink

Structure

Language feature

Orientation

Telling who, where and what

Complication

Something happens which changes princess's life

Princess and Oink

Once upon a time there was a pig called Princess. Princess was a clean pig. She loved to dance, and she sang at the opera. Everybody came to watch her sing.

One day a pig called Oink came to town and heard Princess sing. He said to himself, "She has a marvellous voice." After the concert, Oink went to see Princess, and he gave her some flowers and a box of chocolates. They went out to dinner.

At dinner Oink said, "You sang beautifully tonight. Isn't it hard work to sing?"

Princess replied, "No, all you have to do is sing," and they laughed.

Now after every concert Oink went out with Princess.

One day Oink said, "I want to marry you."

Princess replied, "Yes, I want to marry you, too."

It all goes well for a while but a worse complication

So they married. But Princess found out that Oink always went into mud and he was loud and lazy. She had to do it all! She had to clean his shoes, get him dressed, make the bed and a lot more things.

Resolution

Things work out well — in the end.

One day Princess said to her husband, "I won't have it any more!" Then Oink thought how nice he was when they met and said to Princess, "I will help with everything." From then on Oink always helped by cleaning his shoes and making the beds — and he even got her a box of chocolates and flowers and took her out, and they lived happily ever after.

Sam, Year 3

Proper nouns e.g. 'Princess', 'Oink'

Past tense verbs e.g. 'heard', sang 'said', 'laughed'

Exclamation mark to show horror e.g. 'She had to do it all!'

Dialogue (when people talk) make stories funny o more realistic e.g. "I won't ha it any more!"

Writer's Challenge

Narratives often contain dialogue. Quotation ('talking') marks show when people are speaking. Use a red pen to underline all the words in the story which are spoken. (Look for the words which are inside the quotation marks.)

Write a narrative

Oink's story—a different ending

What would have happened if Oink hadn't changed his ways?
What if he had stayed lazy and muddy?

Read the story again and write your own ending. Continue the
story from … One day Princess said… "I won't have it any more!"

You continue

Princess and Oink continued …

One day Princess said "I won't have it any more!"

Write your own 'pig' story. It could be a story about
well-known pigs, or one that is all your own.

The magic cloak: a folk tale from Norway

Structure

Title

Orientation

When?
Who?
Where?

Sequence of events

Resolution

Not a typical ending. Aldar plays a trick on the stranger.

Language featur...

Folk tales are abou ordinary people

Exaggeration ir many folk tales

Past tense verl These are action w They tell us what happened.

Alliteration 'sat up straigh in his saddle'

Talking marks used for speec

The Magic Cloak

Once there was a poor young Norwegian boy called Aldar. The only two things he owned in the world were an old lame horse and a cloak with seventy patches and ninety holes.

One snowy winter's day, Aldar was riding sadly along on his half-frozen horse when he spied a rich man with a fox-fur coat on a splendid horse. Aldar sat up straight in his saddle, opened his cloak and began to sing.

The stranger was amazed. "Don't you feel the cold?" he asked. "Not at all," said Aldar. "The wind blows in one hole and out another, so I stay warm. I feel sorry for you in that fox-fur coat. You must be *so* cold."

"Yes, I *do* feel cold," the man agreed. "Would you sell or swap your coat? PLEASE!"

"Mmm, I'm not sure," said Aldar. "Oh, very well. I'll swap coats if we exchange horses as well!"

"Done! It's a deal!" cried the man.

Aldar slipped on the fox-fur coat and galloped away on the splendid horse before the stranger had a chance to change his mind.

Writer's Challenge

Numbers for words

Write the numbers next to the words.

1 **The cloak had seventy _____ patches and ninety _____ holes.**

2 **<u>Three</u> bears: _____ ; <u>forty-seven</u> pigs: _____ ; <u>seven</u> dwarfs _____ .**

3 **<u>Twelve</u> dancing princesses: _____ ; <u>one hundred and one</u> dalmations _____ .**

4 **Forty: _____ ; one hundred and seventy-one: _____ ; one hundred and eleven _____ ;**

   one thousand and one _____ ; one thousand and thirty-three: _____ .

Write a narrative

Folk tales

Write your own folk tale. Choose your own characters and places.
Folk tales are different from fairy tales. Fairy tales are magical, but folk tales are about ordinary people (folk like us).
Sometimes, folk tales are TALL tales.

Structure

Title

Orientation

Write a good introduction. Begin 'One day'

Sequence of events

Outline problem to be solved

How is problem solved

How does story end? What happens to characters?

Conclusion

Folk tales do not end 'And they lived happily ever after'.

Imagine that your folk tale has been published as a picture-story book. In your writing book, design a cover for your book. It must have a front cover and a blurb for the back cover.

Nan

Structure

Title

Setting

Who? What?

Sequence of events

Ending

Author

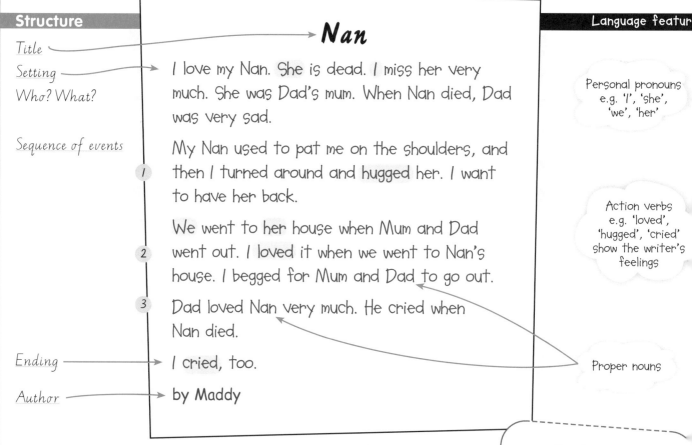

Nan

I love my Nan. She is dead. I miss her very much. She was Dad's mum. When Nan died, Dad was very sad.

1 My Nan used to pat me on the shoulders, and then I turned around and hugged her. I want to have her back.

2 We went to her house when Mum and Dad went out. I loved it when we went to Nan's house. I begged for Mum and Dad to go out.

3 Dad loved Nan very much. He cried when Nan died.

I cried, too.

by Maddy

Personal pronouns e.g. 'I', 'she', 'we', 'her'

Action verbs e.g. 'loved', 'hugged', 'cried' show the writer's feelings

Proper nouns

For the teacher

In this information narrative events and feelings are mixed up and are not in time order. This text is about feelings and memories.

Writer's Challenge

Proper nouns always begin with a capital letter, and name a particular person, place or thing. The answers to the questions below are all proper nouns.

1 What is the title of the information narrative?_____

2 Who is the author?_____

3 Who went out?_____

4 Who was sad?_____

Write an information narrative

Someone special or something special

Write a HAPPY information narrative. Think of a VERY SPECIAL person you know. Write some things you remember about her or him, or you might like to write about something very special which happened to you. Remember to write about your feelings.

Think about your very favourite place. Write about it in your writing book. Where is it? Why do you like it? Who goes there? How do you feel when you are in your favourite place?

A poem about the senses

Structure

Title

Verse 1

Line 1 is repeated in each verse

Lines 2 and 4 rhyme in each verse

Verse 2

Verse 3

Verse 4

Verse 5

Poet

Walking through the zoo

You be the artist. Draw funny small pictures for each verse.

Walking through the zoo.
What is that I see?
It is a rhino!
Staring straight at me.

Walking through the zoo.
What is that I hear?
It is a lion!
Roaring in my ear.

Walking through the zoo.
What is that I smell?
It is the monkeys!
They don't smell well.

Walking through the zoo.
What is that I feel?
It is a parrot!
Nibbling at my heel.

Walking through the zoo.
What is that I say?
I am coming back...
Another day!

Anon.

Anon. is short for ANONYMOUS, which means the author is not known.

Writer's Challenge

Go on a class trail. Work with your teacher. One person is blindfolded, your friend is the helper. You have to go round, over, across, under things in the school ground without getting hurt. After you have both had a turn, write about how it felt. It might be a poem, or it might just be a description of your feelings.

Write a poem

A poem about the senses

Some of the lines of the poem have been written. Write in the words for the missing lines. Remember, the poem is about what you see and hear and smell and feel and say in the bush.

Structure

Title

Walking through the bush

Verse 1

Walking through the bush
What do I see?

You write this line

birds
flowers   trees
bright insects
butterflies

A twig and a bee.

Verse 2

Walking through the bush
What do I hear?

You write this line

buzzing bees
calling birds
whistling wind
crunching leaves

Loud and clear.

Verse 3

Walking through the bush
What do I smell?

You write this line

eucalyptus leaves
fresh air and leaves
teatree smells
honey blossom

An old egg shell.

Verse 4

Walking through the bush
What do I feel?

You write these lines

dripping water
creeping branches
prickly thorns
leaves underneath

Verse 5

Walking through the bush
What do I say?

You write these lines

shout loud
whisper
talk to the birds
'Hip, hip, hooray!'

Poet
(your name)

More to do

In your writing book, write your own poem. It could be another poem about the senses. For example, 'Walking in the city', 'Walking by the seaside' or it could be a different kind of poem.

Things

The poem below is modelled on a poem (also called 'Things') by William Jay Smith.

This poem was written by Peter Meade when he was in Grade 4 at Montrose Primary School in Victoria.

Structure

Title

4 lines that rhyme

The last line in each verse is the same

Poet

Language featur

The syllables or sound parts each line give t poem its rhyth

Rhyming words

Repetition of the last lin gives it added importance

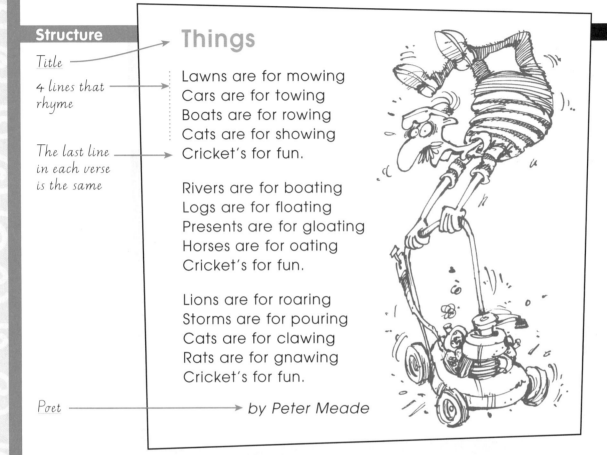

Things

Lawns are for mowing
Cars are for towing
Boats are for rowing
Cats are for showing
Cricket's for fun.

Rivers are for boating
Logs are for floating
Presents are for gloating
Horses are for oating
Cricket's for fun.

Lions are for roaring
Storms are for pouring
Cats are for clawing
Rats are for gnawing
Cricket's for fun.

by Peter Meade

Writer's Challenge   Time for a rhyme

Write rhymes for:

sigh _____ _____ _____

when _____ _____ _____

sea _____ _____ _____

silly   *thrilly**   _____ _____

* Sometimes it is **sunny** to **shake up** some **birds**.
  funny   make up   words

Write a poem

Things

Write your own 'Things' poem, modelled on the one on the left-hand page. Illustrate it with 'Things' from your poem.

Remember rhythm and rhyme

← Write your title here

by

Write your name here

Publish your poem beautifully on A4 paper and cover paper, and make a class book of 'Things' poems to share and enjoy.

Writer's word list

a	didn't	I'm	off	they
about	do	if	oh	thing
after	dog	in	old	think
again	don't	into	on	this
all	door	is	one	thought
also	down	it	only	three
always	eat	its	or	time
am	ever	just	other	to
an	every	know	our	told
and	father	left	out	too
another	finally	like	over	took
any	find	little	people	two
are	first	long	play	up
around	for	look	put	us
as	found	made	ran	very
asked	friend	make	really	wanted
at	friends	man	red	was
away	from	many	right	water
back	fun	me	room	we
be	get	money	said	well
because	go	moon	saw	went
bed	going	more	say	were
before	good	morning	school	what
best	got	most	see	when
boy	had	mother	she	where
brother	has	Mr	should	while
but	have	much	so	white
by	heard	mum	some	who
called	help	my	something	why
came	her	name	started	will
can	here	never	stitches	wish
car	him	new	take	with
children	his	next	tell	work
colour	home	nice	that	world
could	house	night	the	would
couldn't	how	no	them	year
Dad	I	not	then	years
day	I'd	now	there	you
did	I'll	of	these	your

What I think about my writing

My writing goals (TO BE COMPLETED AT THE START OF THE YEAR)

Things I can do

JUNE

DECEMBER

Things I need to improve

JUNE

DECEMBER

Student's writing profile

INDICATORS	E	C	B	N
1 Recounts				
• Understands that recounts can record events and can re-tell personal experiences				
• Understands that recounts include diaries, news reports, journals, biographies				
• Provides details of setting/environment				
• Interprets events imaginatively and elaborates the most important				
• Elaborates aspects of character in relation to events				
• Develops character by use of dialogue or important actions				
• Sustains recount topic throughout				
• Writes a concluding statement that summarises/evaluates the recount				
• Maintains past tense				
• Uses varied conjunctions and linking time words				
• Groups related sentences into paragraphs				
2 Transactions				
• Writes simple notes to friends				
• Attempts simple letters				
• Attempts simple invitations				
• Discusses the purpose of simple surveys and questionnaires				
3 Reports				
• Understands that reports provide information				
• Writes an introduction with a generalisation/classification				
• Includes some detailed, accurate description of the report subject				
• Elaborates upon special features of subject				
• Makes relevant comparisons to aid in visualising the subject				
• Uses paragraphs to organise information				
• Uses specific vocabulary related to subject				
• Maintains timeless present tense				
• Uses linking verbs and timeless action verbs effectively				
• Writes a concluding paragraph that includes the main aspects of the report				
4 Procedures				
• Demonstrates understanding of the range of purposes for written procedures				
• States goal in precise language				
• Lists materials required under heading and uses appropriate layout				
• States method/instructions in detail and in correct sequence				
• Uses diagrams and labels to support text				
• Refers to classes of things as well as specific things within that class				
• Uses action words to begin steps in procedure				
• Maintains simple present tense				
• Uses linking words such as 'next', 'after'				

INDICATORS		CODE		
	E	C	B	NA
5 Persuasive texts				
• Writes an introduction that provides content for the argument following				
• Provides adequate information in a logical, systematic way				
• Attempts some generalisation				
• Includes some personal judgements about the topic				
• Attempts a summarising paragraph that re-states/reinforces the position adopted				
• Makes effective use of conjunctions such as 'too', 'also', 'although', 'however'				
6 Explanations				
• Recognises that explanations explain how things work, and provides reasons for phenomenon				
• Includes information in a logical sequence				
• Explains links between cause and effect				
• Uses cause and effect linking words, e.g. 'if', 'when', 'why'				
• Uses simple present tense consistently				
• Uses passive voice, e.g. 'is caused by'				
• Uses a range of subject-specific terms				
7 Narratives				
• Understands that stories are written for a variety of reasons (to entertain, teach, inform etc.)				
• Chooses a suitable title				
• Includes details of time, place and characters to establish context				
• Uses detailed description of characters				
• Includes events which develop into complications				
• Uses environment to build suspense				
• Attempts to tie together events in order to provide a satisfying conclusion				
Resolves conflicts in the story				
• Uses some similes, metaphors and imagery to add interest				
• Uses a variety of sentence lengths to change tempo of writing				
8 Writing strategies				
• Uses other texts as models for own writing				
Adds to/improves writing in response to suggestions from peers, teachers, helpers				
Presents writing in a legible and attractive format appropriate for the audience				
Attempts new words in writing, even though unsure of correct spelling				
Identifies and corrects errors in known spelling, using a variety of strategies and resources				
Checks drafts for meaning and correct use of writing conventions				

Text Types for Primary Schools

FACTUAL TEXTS

	BOOK 1	BOOK 2	BOOK 3	BOOK 4	BOOK 5	BOOK 6
Recount	• What I did yesterday • I remember crying • I went on a picnic • I like hearing the crickets • My special place	• The big fish • The new playground • Dog in the fridge • I fell in the river	• A visit to the zoo • Stitches in my head • A school excursion: the bird-walk • The day our duck egg hatched	• Our mud fight • It still makes my blood boil … • The day we left Jack behind	• A day in my life • The slug • A brush with a shark • A newspaper report: Camel fiasco a laughing matter	• Why me? • Stuck in the middle again! • Talking about me — a personal recount • A newspaper report: TV zaps memory
Transaction	• A party invitation • A thank-you letter	• A birthday card • A letter from Virginia	• A letter to the Kids' Council	• A letter to Mr Pasini	• Invitation to join a music club	• A letter of agreement
Report	• How lemonade is made • Wasps • The robin	• The shapes of leaves • From sheep to jumper • Butterflies • Chickens	• Sharks • Dinosaurs • Polar bears • Bread • Our axolotl	• Lions • Tyrannosaurus • Mummies • ASIMO the robot	• Praying Mantis • Jupiter • Muscles	• Insect-eating plants • The Internet • From egg to tadpole to toad
Procedure	• How to make orange jelly • How to make a leaf rubbing • How to make mud bricks • How to make a fruit salad	• How to grow trees on tiny islands • How to make a floating flower • How to make a green hairy head • How to play Scissors, Paper, Rock	• Making a pizza • How to make mud pies • How to make pepper jump	• Yeast power • Pirate's treasure map • Making a worm farm	• How to make a compost bin in a soft drink bottle • Maps and directions • The four torn edges	• How to make a shadow puppet • How to make worm fritters • How to have a bath
Persuasive	• "I like …" • A sunsmart poster	• What we need in the world • Ice creams • Kangashoos	• Homework! Yes or no? • Cats make good pets • Poster: Cracklin' burgers	• Spaghetti • Sun bars	• Letter to a magazine • Bush dance poster	• A national disgrace • The coach's address • I think I'll become a vegetarian • Writing an advertisement
Explanation	• How does a plant grow? • How do spiders spin webs?	• Why are birds' beaks different? • Why do birds sing?	• Why can you see your breath on a cold day? • Why do moths flutter around lamps? • What are fossils?	• How are rainbows formed? • Why do stars twinkle? • Why do we feel dizzy when we spin around?	• What causes earthquakes? • Where does food go? • What causes thunder and lightning?	• Why do leaves change colour in autumn? • What causes the doldrums? • What is a red giant?
Biography			• Alice Grant — circus star	• Alexander Selkirk — marooned sailor	• Bert Facey — a "fortunate" man	• Mary Kingsley — African adventurer

LITERARY TEXTS

	BOOK 1	BOOK 2	BOOK 3	BOOK 4	BOOK 5	BOOK 6
Narrative	• The lion and the mouse • The scared elf • Two stories • The poor woman's wish	• The magic horse • Albert the dinosaur • The seed that grew • The fox and the stork: a fable	• The ants and the grasshopper • Princess and Oink • The magic clock: a folk tale from Norway	• A Norwegian myth • The sick camel • On the way to school • Prunella Pelican	• A Greek legend • The possum chase • The farmer and his sons	• Tourist eats crocodile • The starfish story • Around the bend
Information narrative			• Nan	• My shed • Holiday at Pickering's Hut	• My pop • Along the river track	• Where do writers get their ideas?
Poetry	• Jump or jiggle • Wishes • Quiet is …	• My dreams • Beans, beans, beans • Autumn leaves	• A poem about the senses • Things	• Word pictures • Over and under • Dirbs and gorfs	• He was … • Acrostics • What is … a million?	• Why? • Landscape • That was summer